I Am Smart!

Knowing Your Strengths

Miriam Phillips

SOCIAL AND EMOTIONAL LEARNING FOR THE REAL WORLD™

Rosen Classroom™

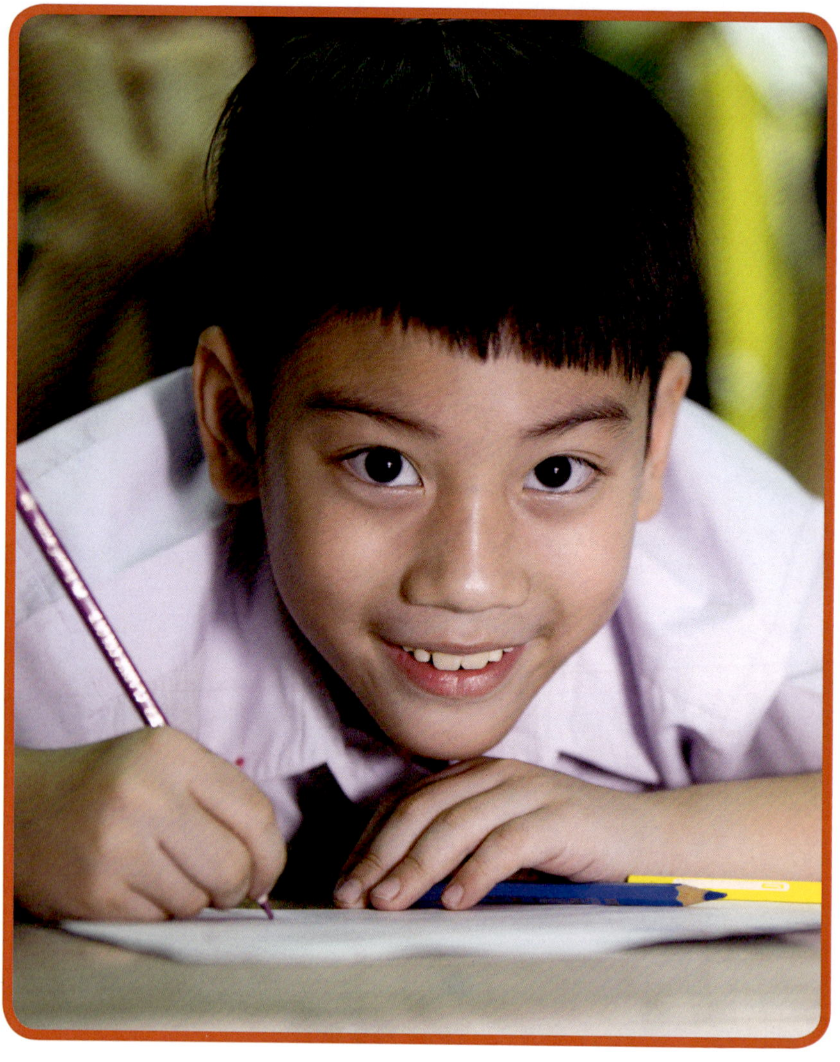

I am smart.

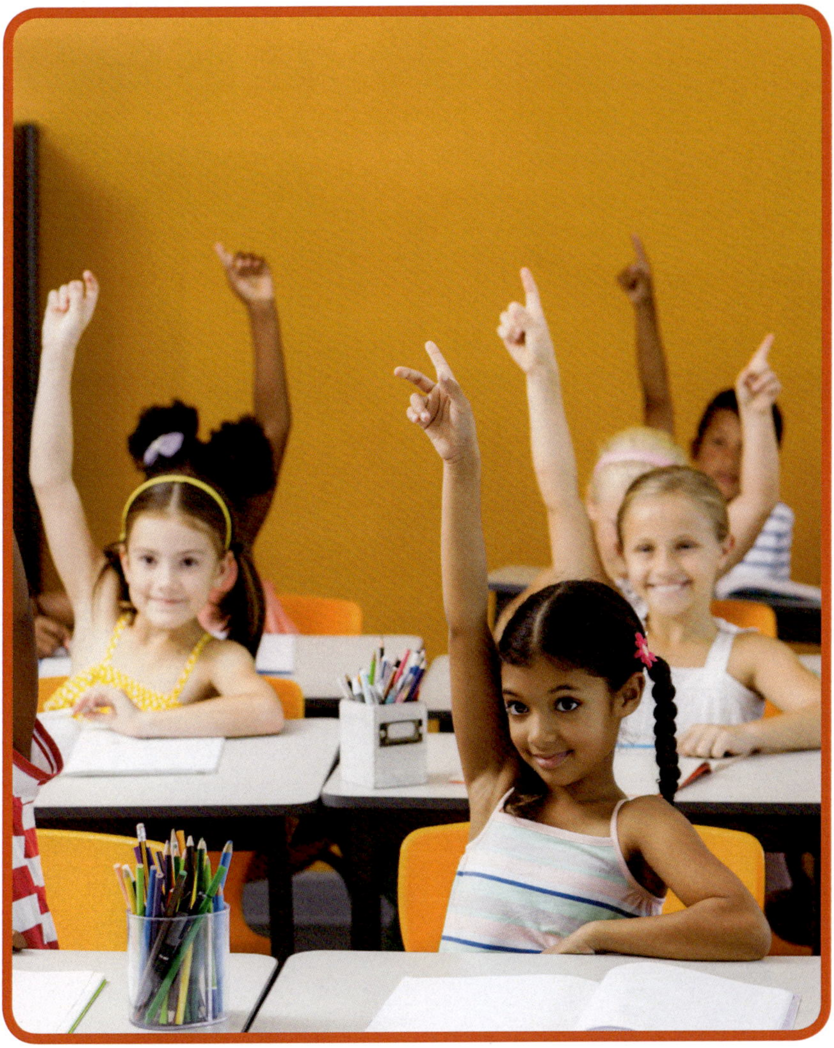

I know a lot.

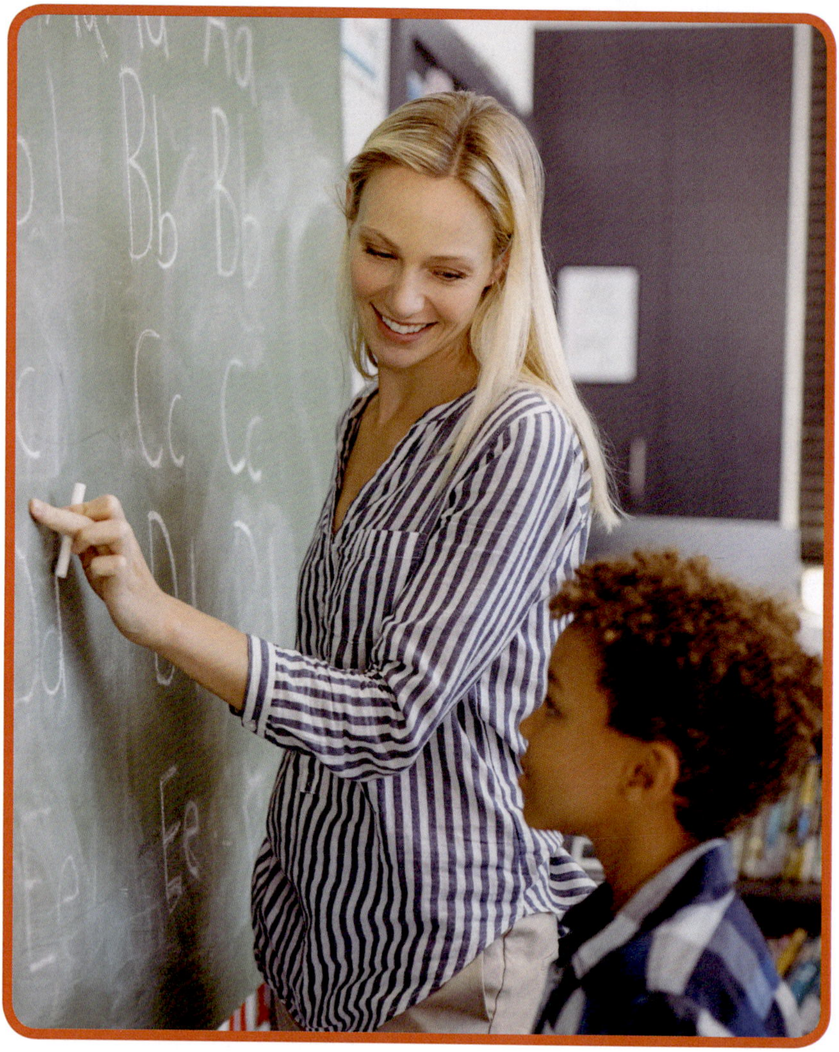

I know letters.

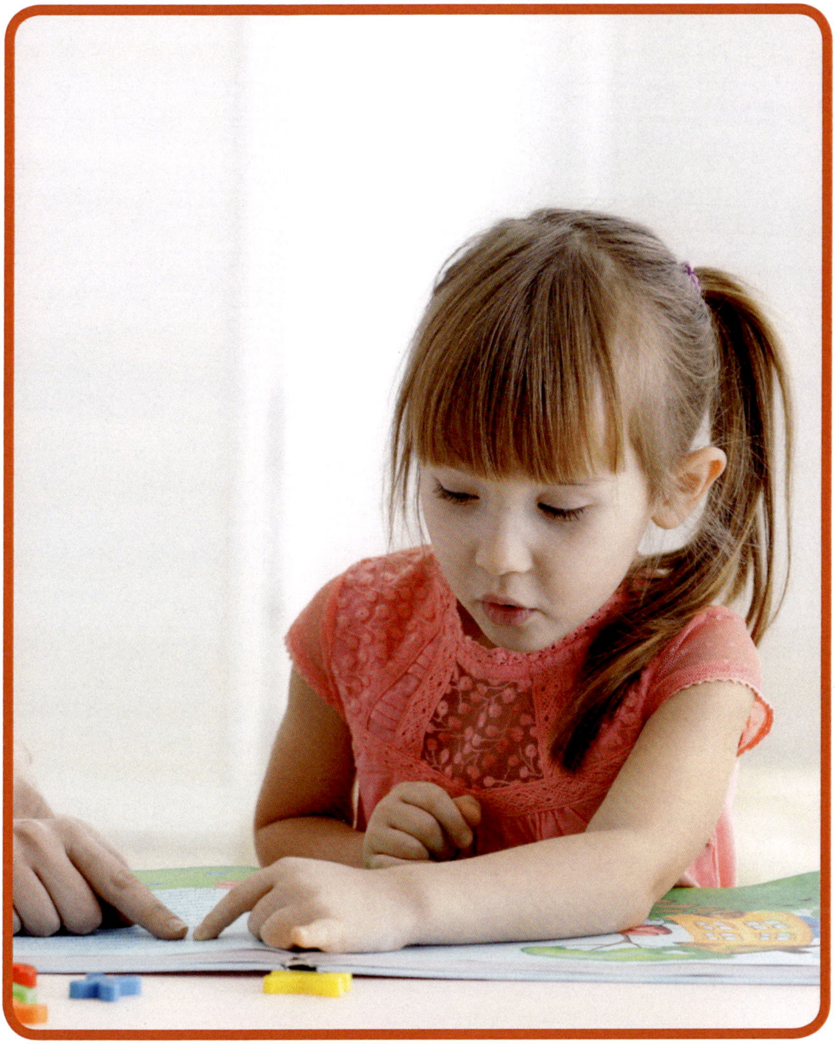

I know sounds.

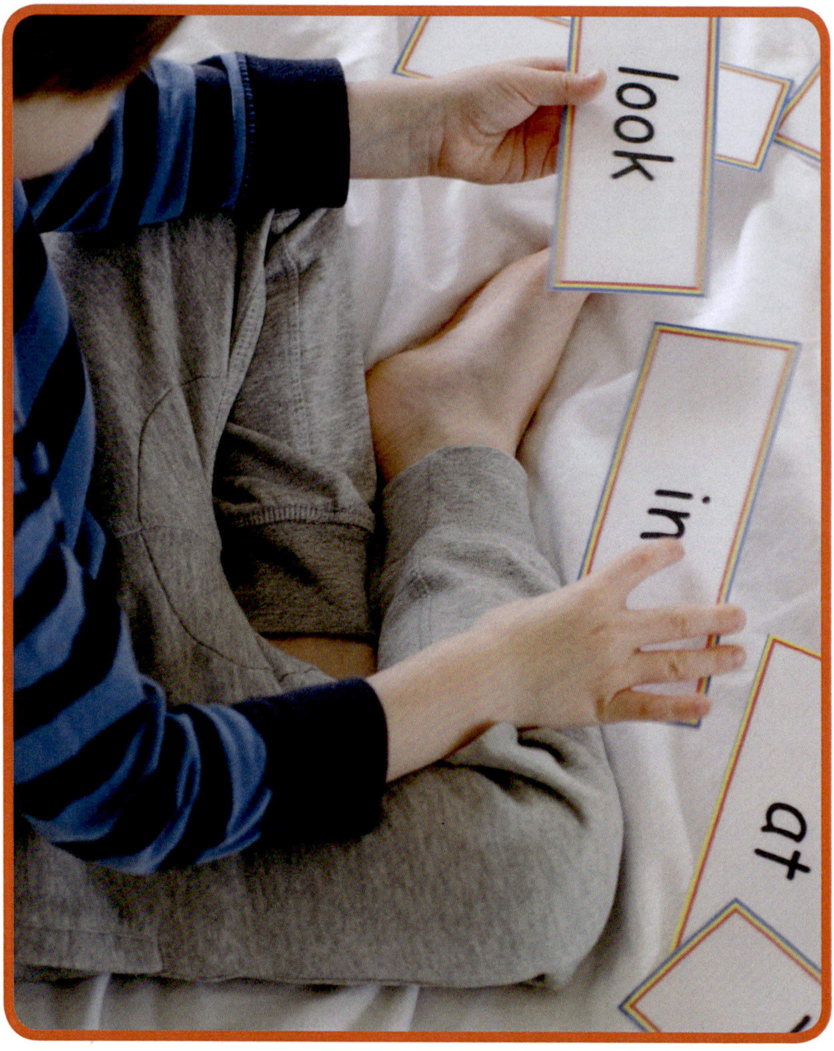

I know words.

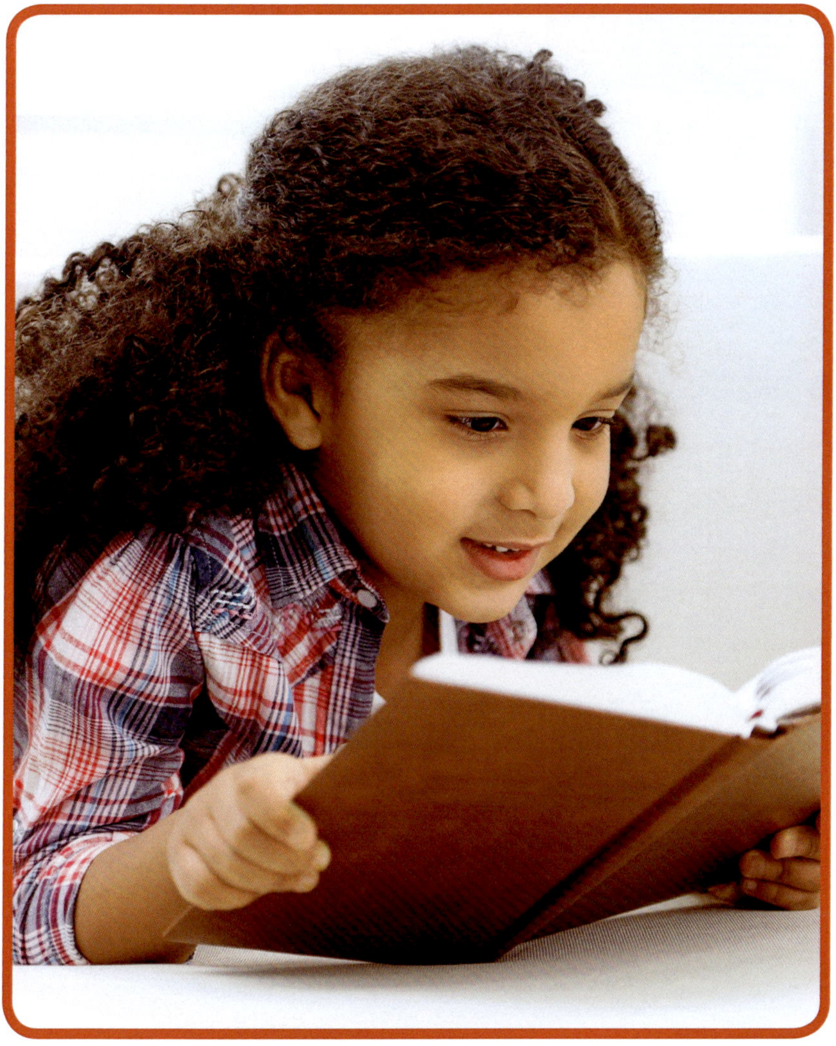

I know how to read.

Words to Know

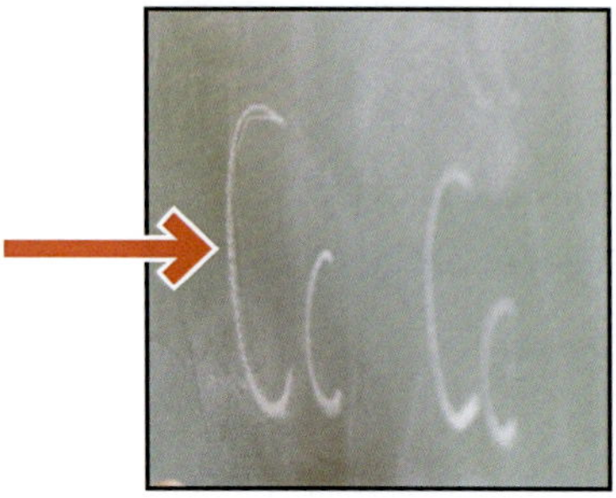

letter

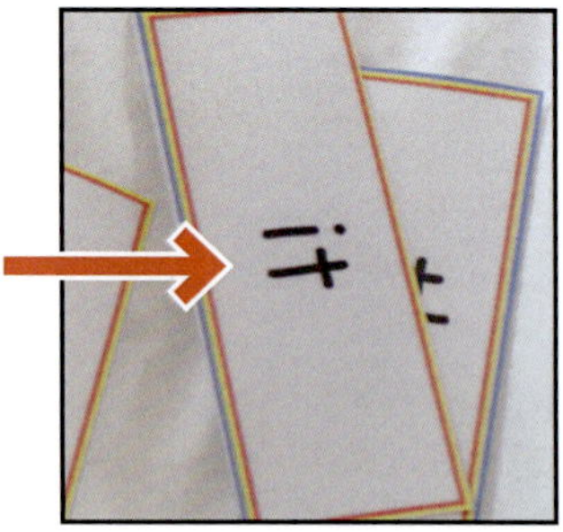

word